Easy Peasy
lemon
SQUEEZY

Find our books at Amazon, Barnes & Nobles, Walmart, Books-A-Million, OverDrive, Kobo, Lulu and more!

Like, Share and Follow us on Facebook, Instagram, Twitter, Pinterest, YouTube, LinkedIn, Spotify, Apple Podcast and more!

www.SlothDreamsBooks.com

Published by Sloth Dreams Books & Publishing, LLC.
Sloth Dreams Children's Books
Pennsylvania, USA
www.SlothDreamsBooks.com

ISBN: 978-4-1729-6867-2

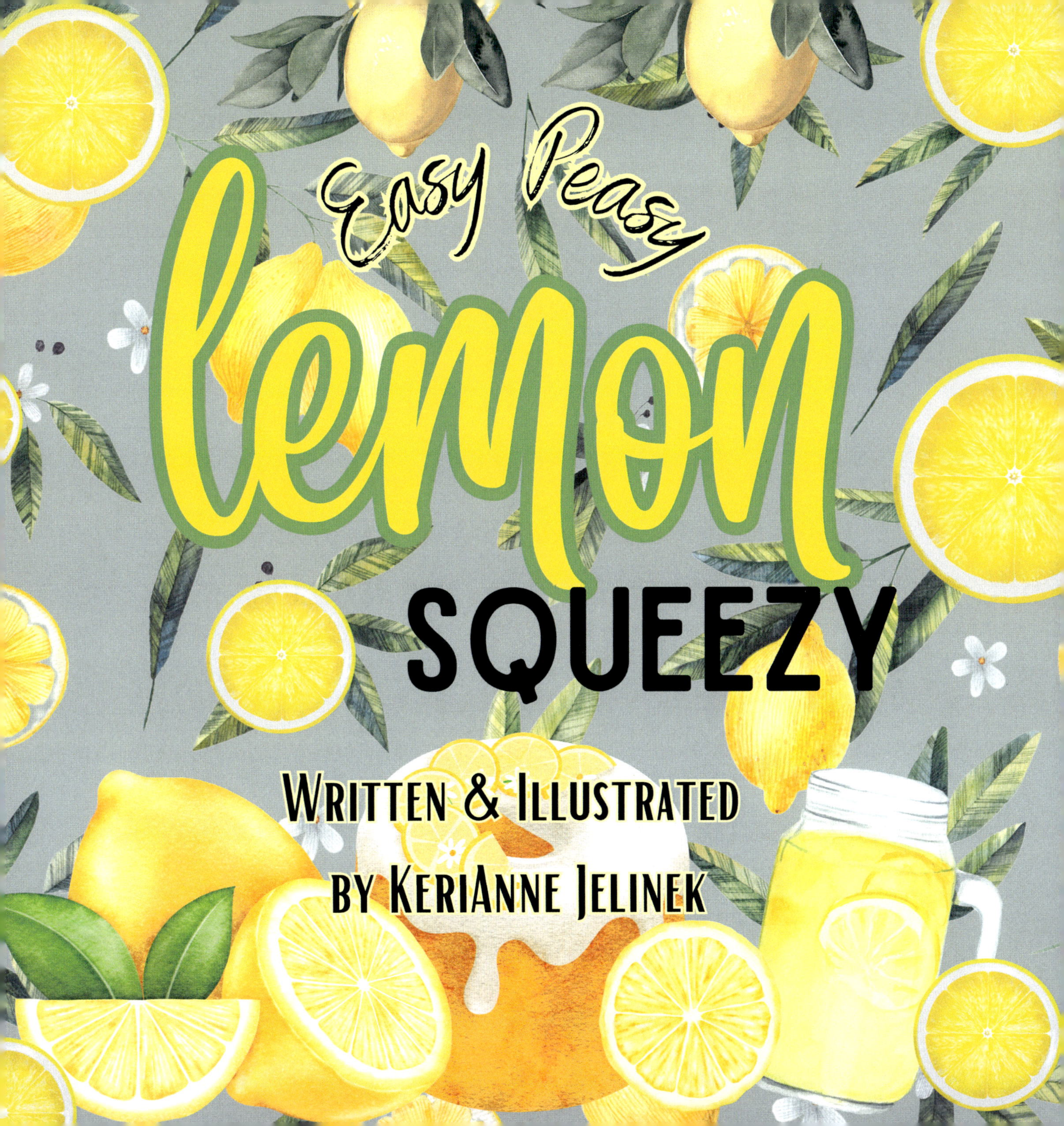
Easy Peasy
lemon
SQUEEZY
Written & Illustrated
by KeriAnne Jelinek

LEMONS ARE YELLOW AND OH SO BRIGHT,
THEY FILL OUR SENSES WITH SUCH DELIGHT!

JUICY AND TANGY, THEY MAKE US SMILE,
LEMONS ARE A TREAT, NO MATTER THE STYLE!

Lemonade
Lemonade

WITH JUST A SQUEEZE, LEMON JUICE APPEARS,
A VERSATILE FRUIT, THAT'S SO VERY DEAR!

LEMONADE IN THE SUMMER,
A REFRESHING DRINK,
COOL AND SWEET, IT'S JUST WHAT
WE WANT TO DRINK!

Lemonade

LEMON BREAD IS ANOTHER TREAT,
MOIST AND FLUFFY, IT CAN'T BE BEAT!

ADD SOME ZEST, AND THE FLAVOR WILL SOAR,
IT'S EASY PEASY, YOU'LL WANT SOME MORE!

LEMON CHICKEN, A SAVORY DISH,
A TANGY FLAVOR THAT YOU CAN'T RESIST!

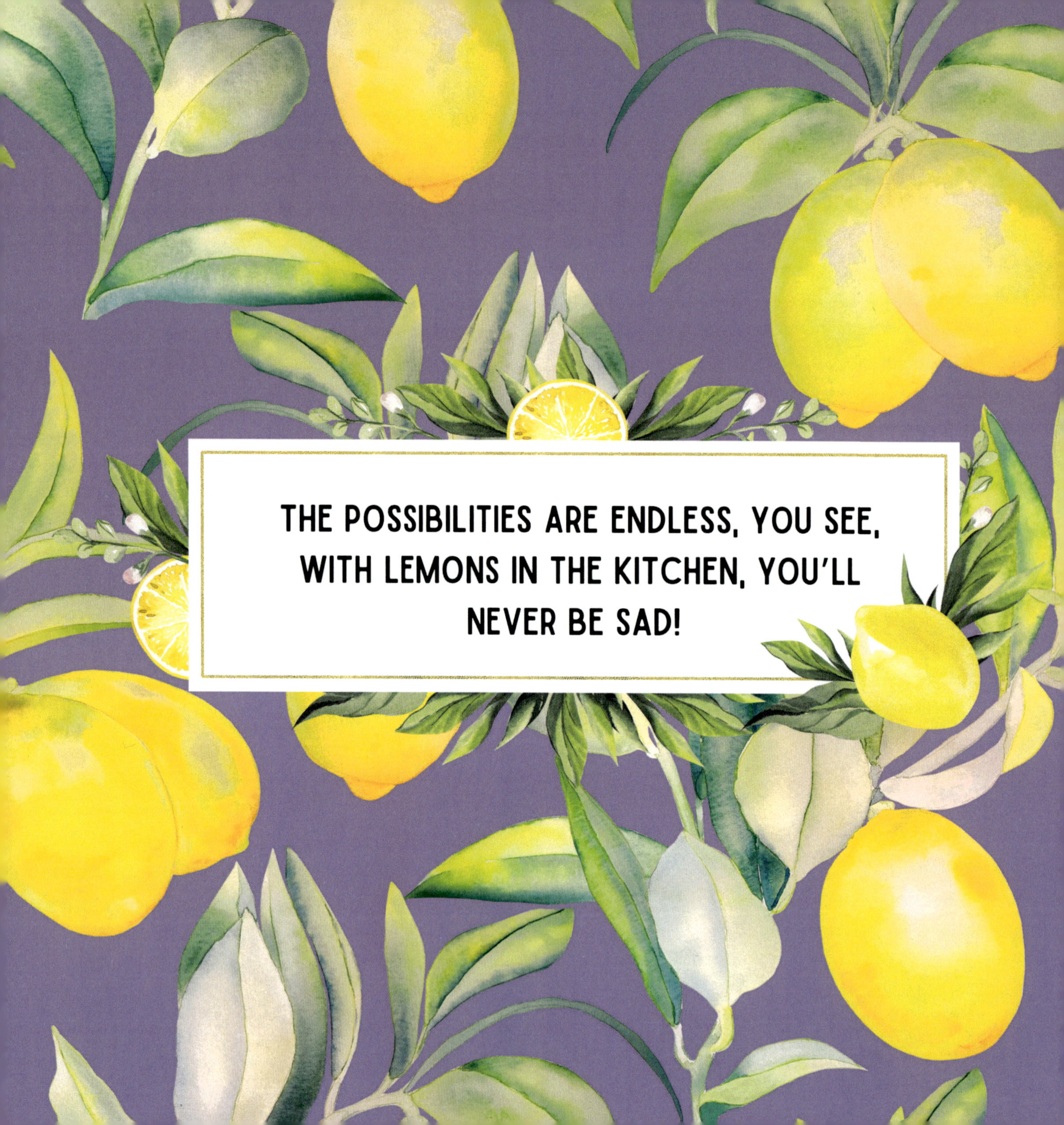
THE POSSIBILITIES ARE ENDLESS, YOU SEE,
WITH LEMONS IN THE KITCHEN, YOU'LL
NEVER BE SAD!

BUT WHERE DO LEMONS COME FROM,
YOU MIGHT ASK?
THEY GROW ON TREES, A CITRUS TASK!

WARM WEATHER AND SUNSHINE,
JUST WHAT THEY NEED,
TO GROW AND THRIVE, FROM JUST
A SMALL SEED.

LEMONS ARE SPECIAL, IN THEIR OWN WAY,
A VERSATILE FRUIT, THEY BRIGHTEN EVERY
SINGLE DAY!

I LIKE THE FLAVOR OF LEMON CHIFFON
AND I EAT IT UNTIL IT'S ALL GONE!

EASY PEASY LEMON SQUEEZY,
WE SAY WITH GLEE,
LEMONS ARE A JOY, FOR YOU AND ME!

Lemonade
Tip Jar

SO EMBRACE THE MAGIC OF LEMONS, BIG AND SMALL, LET THEIR BRIGHT ESSENCE UPLIFT AND ENTHRALL, FOR IN THE WORLD OF FLAVORS, THEY REIGN SUPREME, EASY PEASY LEMON SQUEEZY!

Lemonade

Strawberry Lemonade

Ingredients:

1 cup fresh strawberries, hulled and sliced

1/2 cup freshly squeezed lemon juice (about 4-5 lemons)

4 cups cold water

1/4 cup granulated sugar (adjust to taste)

Ice cubes

Fresh mint leaves (optional, for garnish)

Instructions:

Wash the strawberries thoroughly under cold water. Remove the green stems and slice the strawberries into small pieces.

In a blender or food processor, puree the strawberries until smooth. If your child prefers a smoother texture, you can strain the puree to remove any seeds, but this step is optional.

In a pitcher, combine the freshly squeezed lemon juice, cold water, and sugar. Stir well until the sugar is completely dissolved.

Add the strawberry puree to the pitcher and stir again until well combined. Taste the mixture and adjust the sugar according to your child's preference. Add more sugar if desired.

Fill serving glasses with ice cubes and pour the strawberry lemonade over the ice.

If desired, garnish each glass with a sprig of fresh mint leaves for added flavor and visual appeal.

Stir the lemonade before serving to ensure that the strawberry puree is evenly distributed.

Serve the strawberry lemonade chilled and enjoy!

Note: You can involve your child in the process by letting them help with washing the strawberries, squeezing the lemons, or stirring the mixture. It can be a fun and educational activity for them!

Made in United States
Orlando, FL
23 April 2024

46105731R00022